TABLE OF CONTENTS

SPRING SALAD	3
RETRO SNACKS	15
CARROT VICHYSSOISE	17
PUMPKIN SOUP	19
VEGETABLE SOUP WITH MEATBALLS	21
PARSNIP SOUP WITH CHAMPIGNONS	23
SCALLOPS WITH PARSNIP CRÈME	25
BRUSCHETTA	27
RAVIOLI WITH RICOTTA AND BUTTER SAGE SAUCE	29
MARROW FAT PEA STEW	31
SWEET POTATO SHEPHERD'S PIE	33
ARTICHOKE PASTA	35
PENNE ALL'ARRABIATA	37
CHICK PEA AND LENTIL CURRY	39
KALE AND SMOKED SAUSAGE	41
SALSA AL POMODORO	43
PAPRIKÁS KRUMPLI	45
KEDGEREE	47
KOHLRABI GALA APPLE CLAMS	49
GAMBAS AL AJILLO	51
RATATOUILLE	53
INDIAN CURRY	55
BARBECUED STUFFED DORADE	57
BANANA BREAD	59
CHOCOLATE CAKE WITH MINIMUM EFFORT	61
ILLUSTRATE YOUR OWN FAVORITE RECIPE!	63

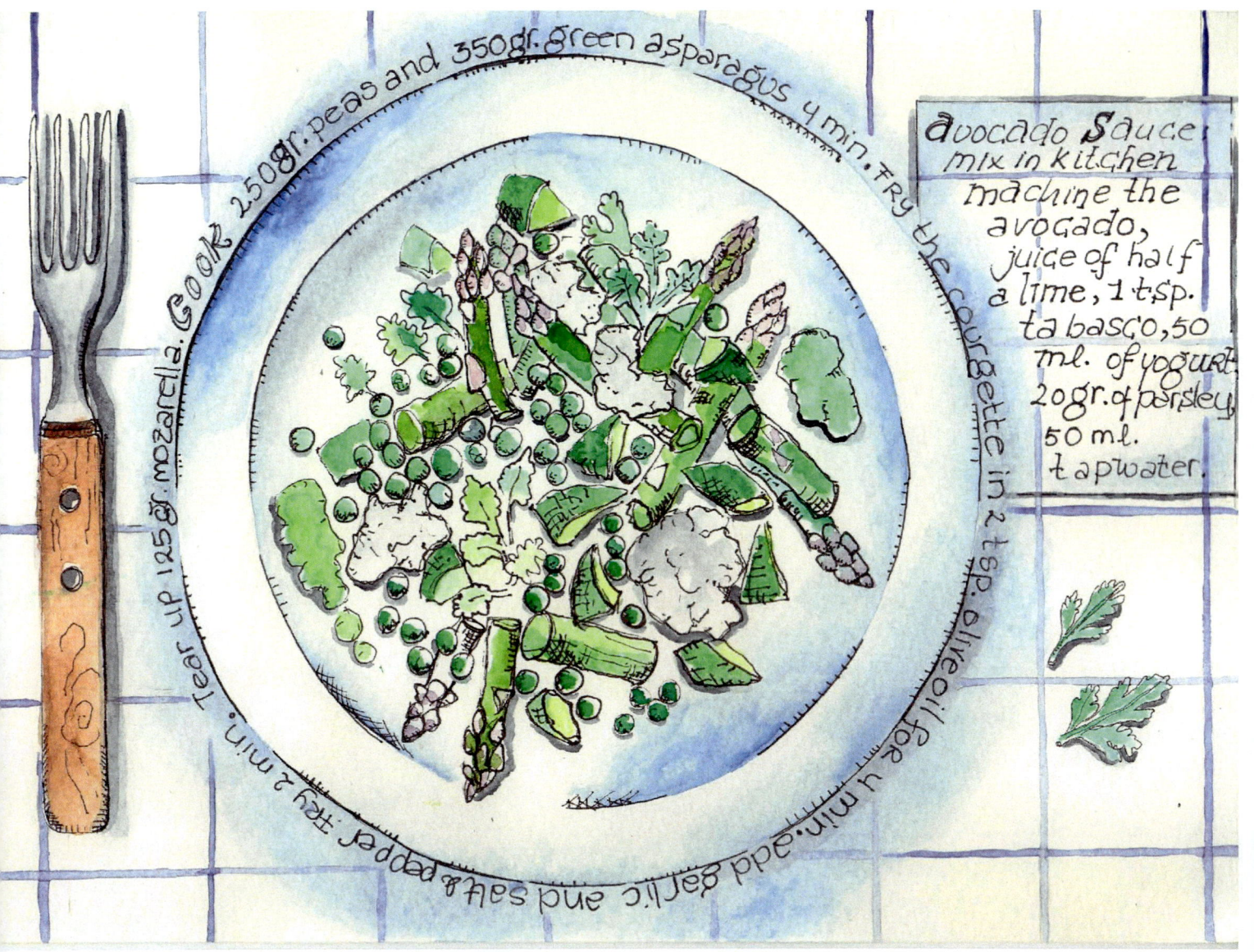

Cook 250gr. peas and 350gr. green asparagus 4 min. Fry the courgette in 2 tsp. olive oil for 4 min. Add garlic and salt & pepper. Fry 2 min. Tear up 125gr. mozarella.

Avocado Sauce: mix in kitchen machine the avocado, juice of half a lime, 1 tsp. tabasco, 50 ml. of yogurt, 20 gr. of parsley, 50 ml. tapwater.

SPRING SALAD

FENNEL

CAPERS OLIVES

FENNEL WITH CAPERS AND OLIVES

lemon juice

4 tsps of olive oil

2 tsps pine seeds
2 tsps olives

2 tsps of capers

3 fennel bulbs in slices

Preheat oven at 220 C. Arrange the fennel slices on a baking tray. Sprinkle with olive oil, salt & pepper, capers and olives. Bake in oven for about 15 min.

Finish with pine seeds and lemon juice. Serve with fish!

AUBERGINE AND MACKEREL SALAD

Cut 1 kohlrabi and 1 carrot in small sticks. Dipsauce: whisk 1 egg yolk, 1 tsp. mustard and some apple vinegar in a bowl. Slowly work in 100 ml. mild olive oil until you have a good mayonnaise. Turn in some yogurt and chive halms cut small.

KOHLRABI CARROT STICKS

Organic salami/gherkin and cocktail onion snack.

RETRO TREAT

RETRO SNACKS 15

Vichyssoise - Carol

Cold soup

Shopping list:
- 125 gr. crème fraîche
- 4 medium potatoes, peeled, cut in cubes
- 4 medium leeks, use white only, sliced
- 1 big carot, peeled, cut in slices
- 1 ltr. chicken broth
- 2 tsp of butter
- chives, chopped fine

Fry leeks and carot until soft
Add chicken broth and potatoes, boil until it cooks
Simmer for 20 min.
Blend in food processor
Add crème fraîche
Season with salt and pepper
Cook for 5 min., stir well
Cool in fridge
Serve with chopped chives

Vegetable Soup with Meatballs

a pot of beef stock

a package of vegetables for soup

a clove of garlic

400 gr. of meat balls   (beef mince)

olive oil

Slice the vegetables in small pieces. Gently fry the onions in 2 tsps of olive oil. Squeeze a clove of garlic in the pan. When the onions are soft, add the rest of the vegetables. Stir fry for a few minutes. Add the beef stock, and three times as much water and the meat balls. Let simmer for 20 minutes.

VEGETABLE SOUP WITH MEATBALLS

Parsnip Soup with Champignons / Eggs / Crème Fraîche

1.
- 2 tablespoons olive oil: heat in soup pan
- 2 shallots (sliced) + one clove garlic: add and slightly fry
- 400 gram parsnip: peel, make dices, add and fry 2 min.
- 1,5 ltrs vegetable bouillon: add, cook 10 min.
- Blend with hand blender
- Season with salt & pepper

2.
- 4 eggs nearly hard boiled in 6,5 min. Dip in cold water, peel, halve

3.
- 2 tablespoons olive oil: heat in frying pan
- 250 gram of chestnut champignons (quatered): add, fry on medium heat, 4 min.
- One clove garlic: press, fry in 1 min.

4.
- 125 gram of crème fraîche, season with salt & pepper

Finally
Divide soup into 4 soup bowls. Distribute the champignons and egg halves. Top with some crème fraîche.

PARSNIP SOUP WITH CHAMPIGNONS

Scallops with a Parsnip Crème
Starter for 4

- 12 scallops
- 4 parsnips
- 500 ml. milk
- 1 red chili
- Clove of garlic
- 2 cm. fresh ginger (peeled and sliced)
- Small onion
- 100 ml. cream
- Salt & pepper
- Butter
- Lemon
- 9 year old fermented vinegar (optimal)
- (Parsley for decoration)

Method:

1. Peel the parsnips. For decoration cut with a Chinese mandolin or cheese slicer 12 discs from the thickest section of the parsnip. Save.
2. Put the garlic, ginger, peeled onion, chili sliced in half, and the diced parsnips in a saucepan with the milk and boil over medium heat until soft.
3. Strain the parsnips and save the milk. Discard the chili, garlic and onion. With a hand mixer liquidize the parsnips adding a little milk to achieve a smooth purée. Work the parsnip through a sieve for a smooth crème.
4. Heat the oven to 200 °C. Lightly oil the parsnip discs, rub each one with a clove of garlic and lay them on an oven tray. Sprinkle with cayenne, pepper & salt. Roast until golden and crisp.
5. Fry scallops in a hot pan for 2 minutes each side. Drizzle with a little lemon.
6. Put 1 tablespoon of parsnip crème in middle of a hot plate.
7. Arrange 3 scallops per plate and decorate with parsnip discs. Drizzle balsamic vinegar around crème.

Bruschetta

Toast the slices of bread in the oven. Mix small tomato cubes with dices of onion and garlic, salt & pepper & olive oil. Spread over toasted bread.

Fry mince meat in olive oil.
Add diced onions and squeezed garlic. Fry with a tsp of curry powder.
Add diced red pepper, 3 carrots sliced, broccoli cut in small bits and marrow fat peas. After frying add some water and let simmer for 15 minutes. Season with salt & pepper.

MARROW FAT PEA STEW

Cook 1 kg. (sweet) potatoes in salted water 20 min. Mash with salt/pepper/olive oil. Fry 600 gr. peas and sliced carrots 6 min in olive oil. Fry 400 gr. minced meat in olive oil until well done, season, add garlic and onion cubes. Add a tin of tomato paste and some stock. Put all ingredients in an oven dish. Cook in a preheated oven 180 C, 45 min.

4 artichokes
1 clove garlic
1 tsp. parsley
1 tsp thyme
450 gr. linguine
1/2 lemon juice
salt & pepper

Cut off stems of artichokes. Cook 40 min. Peel leaves off. Scoop soft parts out of leaves with a spoon. Remove fluffy part from harts. Cut harts in small bits.
Fry herbs and garlic in olive oil. Add artichoke parts. Add salt & pepper & lemon juice.
Serve mixture with linguine.

ARTICHOKE PASTA

Kale/Smoked Sausage

Peel and dice the potatoes. Remove stems from kale, chop leaves, rinse. Boil potatoes and kale in salted water for 20 min. Smash the potatoes, kale, butter, milk, salt & pepper. Heat the sausage as instructed. Serve with gravy, sambal or mustard.

Ingredients:
- 3 cloves of garlic, squeezed.
- 4 tsp olive oil, extra virgin.
- 2 tsp basil leaves, torn.
- 600 gr tomatoes, peeled and cut in cubes.
- sea salt & freshly ground pepper.
- 600 gr dried pasta.

Method:
Put oil & garlic in pan. Gently fry until garlic is golden brown. Add tomato cubes and stew 20 min. on low heat. Add salt, pepper & basil. Take off heat. Cook pasta all dente (not too long). Serve with sauce on top.

Variation: add anchovy cut in small parts, capers or parsley to the sauce.

PAPRIKÁS KRUMPLI

- Fry bacon in cubes until crisp.
- Cut onion in small bits and fey in fat of the bacon.
- add garlic and fry as well.
- Take pan from the cooker.
- Add one tablespoon of paprika powder.
- Add potatoes in quarters, paprikas and tomatoes and some salt
- add some water
- cook until potatoes are soft
- add four tablespoons of sour cream.

KEDGEREE

Fry the onion in vegetable oil lightly, add tomatoes and peas. Fry for another 3 min. add curry powder. Stir well. Then add the rice. mix all together thoroughly. and finally add the mackerel and eggs. Stir well. Season with salt and pepper.

Serve with chutney and optional fresh parsley or koriander.

1 smoked mackerel, cleaned

12 clams

2 tsp. grated ginger
150 gr. bean sprouts
150 ml. cream

1 avocado

dill

Peel the apple and slice it in matchstick thin slices. Do the same with the kohlrabi and sprinkle with the lime juice. (Keep for a few hours in the fridge).
Smash the avocado, together with the grated ginger, in a bowl, add the cream, salt & pepper, and mix to a creamy consistency. Make a crème from this mixture by pushing it through a sieve.
Prepare to serve:
Heat a little olive oil in a pan and sauté the clams for 1 minute each side, add a little unsalted butter at the last minute. Take off the heat.
Heat a little olive oil in another pan and stir fry the apple, kohlrabi and bean sprouts for a minutes, add the sliced clams and their cooking juice.
Serve in a deep bowl and sprinkle with the avocado crème. Decorate with a little dill.

KOHLRABI GALA APPLE CLAMS

- 48 raw shrimps (ca. 600 gr.) with tails
- ½ lemon, squeeze
- 4 tsps. of olive oil
- 8 cloves of garlic, crushed
- 6 dried Spanish peppers
- 8 bay leaves, dried

① Heat the oil, the garlic and peppers until the oil begins to sizzle.
② Add shrimps and bay leaves. Cook on both sides for 3 min.
③ Serve with bread. Sprinkle with lemon juice.

GAMBAS AL AJILLO

Barbecued Stuffed Dorade

1. Light the barbecue
2. Wash the Dorade outside and inside with water. Dry with kitchen paper. Score in three places on both sides to speed up the cooking.
3. Rub the fish in the inside and outside with seasoned olive oil.
4. Fill the fish with courgette, tomato, onion and bay leaf.
5. Put the fish in the fish clamp.
6. Grill the fish on both sides on a medium heated barbecue for 10-15 minutes until the fish is well done.
7. Serve with slices of lemon

⟶ 1 courgette sliced

⟶ 5 tsps of seasoned olive oil.

① Preheat oven at 180°C. Grease cake tin and line with baking paper.

Ingredients:
3 bananas
200 gr. wheat flour
50 gr. butter
2 eggs
150 gr. sugar
2 teaspoons of baking powder
125 gr. crème fraîche
salt

② Sieve flour, baking powder and salt.
③ Mix butter sugar with blender. Add eggs one by one. Add crème fraîche.
④ Spoon through flour mixture
⑤ Blend bananas
⑥ Fold in bananas through dough mixture.

CHOCOLATE CAKE WITH MINIMUM EFFORT

SHOP:
- 250 gr. dark chocolate
- 250 gr. unsalted butter
- 115 gr. dark sugar
- 6 eggs
- 4 tablespoons of sifted white flour
- salt
- zest of orange finely chopped

Preheat oven → 190 °C
Grease a 24cm cake tin.

PLACE the chocolate and butter in a sauce pan and melt au Bain Marie (not too hot).

Split the eggs.
Add the sugar and the finely chopped orange zest to the egg yokes and whisk to a creamy consistancy.
Add a pinch of salt to the egg whites and whip until it forms stiff peaks.
Mix the cooled chocolate sauce to the creamed egg yokes.
Fold in the flour. Fold in 1/3 of the egg whites until well combined and then fold in the rest. Do not overwork the mixture.
Pour the mixture into the baking tin and bake for 35 min.
When cooled the chocolate will set. Sprinkle with cacao powder and thin chards of pure chocolate.
Delicious with chantilly cream and fresh raspberries.

ILLUSTRATE YOUR OWN FAVORITE RECIPE HERE!

THEY DRAW & COOK™

The SKETCH-BOOK COOK
by Dorine van der Vloodt
Copyright © 2015 Studio SSS, LLC
All rights reserved, including the right of reproduction in whole or in part in any form.

Conceived, designed and produced by Studio SSS and Dorine van der Vloodt

STUDIO SSS, LLC
Nate Padavick & Salli Swindell
studiosss.tumblr.com

DORINE VAN DER VLOODT
The Hague, Netherlands

Conversions

Common Measurement Equivalents
3 TS = 1 TBS = 1/2 FL OZ
2 TS = 1 FL OZ
4 TS = 2 FL OZ = 1/4 C
8 TBS = 4 FL OZ = 1/2 C
16 TBS = 8 FL OZ = 1 C
16 FL OZ = 2 C = 1 PT
32 FL OZ = 4 C = 2 PT = 1 QT
128 FL OZ = 16 C = 8 PT = 4 QT = 1 G

Volume
1 TS — 5 ML
1 TBS — 15 ML
1/4 C — 59 ML
1 C — 236 ML
1 PT — 472 ML
1 QT — 944 ML
1 G — 3.8 L

Length
1 IN — 2.54 CM
4 IN — 10 CM
6 IN — 5 CM
8 IN — 20 CM
9 IN — 23 CM
10 IN — 25 CM
12 IN — 30 CM
13 IN — 33 CM

Weight/Mass
1/4 OZ — 7 G
1/3 OZ — 10 G
1/2 OZ — 14 G
1 OZ — 28 G
2 OZ — 57 G
3 OZ — 85 G
4 OZ — 113 G
5 OZ — 142 G
6 OZ — 170 G
7 OZ — 198 G
8 OZ — 227 G
9 OZ — 255 G
10 OZ — 284 G
11 OZ — 312 G
12 OZ — 340 G
13 OZ — 369 G
14 OZ — 397 G
15 OZ — 425 G
16 OZ — 454 G

Oven Temperatures
300°F — 150°C
325°F — 165°C
350°F — 180°C
375°F — 190°C
400°F — 200°C
425°F — 220°C
450°F — 230°C
475°F — 245°C

Helpful Formulas
Tablespoons x 14.79 = Milliliters
Cups x 0.236 = Liters
Ounces x 28.35 = Grams
Degrees F − 32 x 5 ÷ 9 = Degrees C
Inches x 2.54 = Centimeters

Made in the USA
San Bernardino, CA
05 September 2017